THE PELICAN AND THE MOONSTAR
(An Exuma Infinite Series Companion)

"...And so it is with the Pelican parent when its babies are starving and in need, it will prick its chest to cause itself to bleed in order to feed its young; thus, without deliberation, nor any lurking doubt, attuned to the welfare of its children, the Pelican will sacrifice its body; its blood. Salvation..."

~ Kevin Mooney

Copyright 2020 © All Rights Reserved.
Kayleigh Mickayla Mooney and Kevin Michael Mooney
For any permissions, including to use or copy, in part or in whole, please contact: **kmmlaw12@gmail.com**

978-0-578-83319-4

Preamble.

The Good Pelican's domain includes the sky and sea and land; blessing these beaches; all of these swooping, sand swirling shapes and dunes and horizons across the earth, including those that ramble across the sea oat sands of Jekyll Island; including the white beaches on Exuma Infinite, glowing turquoise, lightly, from the reflection of the breathing, lapping shallows.

The Good Pelican is, as such, of the sun; purity in love and light; He is ever present with intention, devotion, charity and direction, showing Himself in the eyes and minds and hearts of men and women and children, strolling or playing or in meditative contemplation on the beach. Silently, He swoops over the topography of the sea, seemingly matching the movement of waves, always catching our eyes, perching in our souls.

The MoonStar, She, an indirect light, though a light that illuminates the sky through which the Pelican flies, remains a fixture of devotion as She circles these earthly opportunities; smiling; speaking in words of light; warning, guiding, spreading her loving voice. Kayleigh, you are reflective of the MoonStar Herself; beautiful; regal; loving and brilliant.

In the merge, in the dimensional overlay, under the watchful presence of the MoonStar, I see The Pelican while sitting here with you on our beach on Jekyll Island, coming in from the south, while you, pulling me to my spirit seat on Exuma Infinite see Him glancing over the waves inbound from the east; hence, all presence is known; all dimensions are one; time and space collapse; all truth is revealed. Rejoice. Rejoice. For the Pelican and the MoonStar have spoken, and we, listening, we have heard the glorious story of our path...

PHYSIOLOGUS ALLERGORCAL

"Hineni"

Be blessed in this, Daddy,
For here I am,
In my life ever changing,
Ever active,
Ever present,
In an elevation of light,
The same old Daughter,
The very same child,
Transitioned into the Higher,
In the love of living water,
Where blessings abound;

Be blessed in this, Daddy,
No matter the rage in the struggle,
No matter the pain,
For here I am,
Here I am,
I am here.

"Physiologus Allegorical"

For the betterment of judgment and interpretation divine, in which allegorical accounts, by design, further the intuition of human kind, the attributes upon which these creatures become legend, resonates in the soul fabric so little and passively regarded; hence, the spirit within these beautiful beings, in this regard, the mighty Alexandrian Pelican, a moon, an angel, shed its light, its love, radiating truth and everlasting life; The nonbeliever, heed; the true eyed, behold; she is a Phoenix that rises over a midnight humid beach, reaching, yearning for that Pelican, Our Pelican, who is pleased with her flame.

"The Pelican"

Far above the turquoise infused waters of Exuma Infinite, The Pelican, He glides silently over His domain; a constant presence, a figure like none other that exists; He watches all of his children and all of His creatures;

A grieving Father coming and going on a tiny skiff (I too, though still limited in my humanity am always under his watchful eye), the oceans that live and breathe, the skies with their whispering joy, the whales that maneuver the nebula mangroves of distant galaxies, the faithful loggerheads resting in star field sargassum, jellyfish orbs of sacred fire that dance upon the breeze like sky lanterns, living cords of rainbows and brilliant sun bursts of color, radiance, a lovely beach walker...My Daughter;

The Pelican circles, always circling, His heart attuned to all that transpires in these worlds, His eye steady, His hope an endless universe itself; He banks on heavenly wind and upon the crystal glittering streams of prayers that lift and gather in the breeze and spiral into tangible golden clouds; He is pleased, certainly pleased with many things and many souls, yet specifically, on this flight, attention He has turned to one of His favorite angels, an angel of the highest order, whose compassion and compliance, whose light and love pervade all molecules of matter, each breath of living water, of eternal life, this grand intercessor, this brilliant spirit in whose eyes the Mighty Pelican flies, this lovely beach walker...My Daughter.

"Transforming Life"

And angst, this sunset, erupts like a blooming tsunami,
The colors wash away the tint of the day,
As evening, flush with scarlet bands of humid cloud,
Crash through the arching golden rays,
Out over the ocean…

…That absorbs my wailing cries…

…And euphoric purple mist and emerald spray,
it scatters the tinsel webbing draped into waves,
That echo the signs of transforming life,
As this day nears the birth of this next day.

"Blackish Metallic Purple"

Sun drift below horizon dimension,
Glow,
Flush with royal passion,
Petals, silky vines, gravitate across the night,
Weaving their way through the metal jungle,
Of a man, sagacious and bright,
Were not for the experiences that gather,
He would be effortless in flight,
But for the grief that gathers,
He breathes metallic purple air,
Blackened, burned and dried.

"This Mystic Sea"

It, speak in spirit tongues,
Breathe the ocean air,
That opens up the lungs,
Breathe the ocean here,
As midnight into quiet succumbs,
When the voices awaken,
And the heartstrings of our souls are strung,
Breathe the ocean near,
And hear the mystic voice,
Carried on a sacred tongue.

"Purple Dream Sea"

Minutes to midnight,
A necklace of summer lightning tucked in storms,
Dangles on the horizon in a saintly accord,
Flashing bright fingers of filigree and gold,
In silence that brushes over my feet,
In a steady wind as the dunes erode,
Its powder, in the dry sand, collects,
As I drift, like the grains, into a pleasant lull…

…Nearby nightly waves collapse in the darkness,
Just one hundred yards distant my stance,
Just passed the utility of my human glance,
As the full moon, emerge from the shrouded field of clouds,
Illuminates the beachfront into a spiritual dance,
Awaken the nest tucked deeply high in the sea grass,
Its travelers, in the dry sand, brush over my feet,
One hundred sea turtle babies scampering passed me,
Yearning toward a velvet, violet hue,
Cast by the mystical full moon,
Called by an angel that presents in front of me,
And gestures on her knees to the tiny creatures…

"Come, my friend, come…

…Toward the Purple Dream Sea…"

"On This Holy Night"

Smoky cloud, it glide,
Swirling and blanket earthly night sky,
Watch its shadows seem to cross the glowing Moon,
At least it seems to be so judged with the naked eye,
Yet thousands of miles of separation,
Bar the atmosphere to that of its satellite,
Or could the dimensions be one…

…On this holy night.

"On the Beach After Midnight"

On this beach after midnight,
Watching the great nebula range,
You warmed in joyful blankets of light,
And I wrapped in blankets of traumatic pain,
Listening to the waves,
We listen to our souls as we remain engaged...

...We sit upon this beach after midnight,
Hypnotized by the moons that bind us,
Like the sea and salt entwine us,
Like the dream that we together create,
Tethered in the golds that find us,
A tapestry of light, surround us,
Eternity it conveys,
Its promise though we cannot see the waves,
In each secret the waters pray,
For you and I after midnight,
Alone with the ocean on this precious beach.

"Purpose and Outcome (Midnight Walks)"

At long last, I came to find that, these devotional and intentional long walks on the beach in the middle of the night, sometimes for four or six hours, were not just a chance for me to be with you, my Daughter, but your calculated way of isolating me enough so that you could spend unbridled time with your Father with whom you are in love. Thus, though I am in a physical state and you are now in your spiritual elevated body, we both move towards the other simultaneously. Our dimensions blend.

That is the book of love.

"Hours in the Darkness in the Beach with You"

In the months when the lamps cease by restriction,
And the beach cast no electrical affliction,
The air itself becomes dark,
So dark so that the hidden tapestry of stars,
Emerges from the night sky...

Before the moon rise to amplify the oasis,
Before the moon's light stages dancing shadows,
Of dune lines and sea oat laces,
The air itself remains dark,
So dark that the fields of distant stars,
Purge the night sky...

Until the eyes adjust in the inky stillness,
Until the human eye can filter or fill this,
The air itself reigns with,
The most perfect moment to gain is...

...The authentic moment with oneself;

And here sitting in the dunes adjusting,
And hearing the ocean and the sea oat rustling,
What better place on earth for communion,
To embrace and grow this loving union,
Than here in the darkness of the air itself,
One with you for I am one with myself,
Where we watch the perfect stillness...

...Drifting by.

"At the Edge of All We Know"

At the edge of all we know,
At the last wedged corner toehold,
At the last inch before the drop off,
In a silence broken by the wild ocean;

In that last hours before sunrise,
In a darkness softened by clouds,
And twinkling galaxies,
The rumbling of the brave Atlantic,
Perpetuates life,
In the accompanied hush,
Silk cupped in my ear,
A sea breeze blush,
Rushes steadily through my hair,
Rattling sea oat in the dunes behind me,
Sing for me, my release,
Like a nest of Loggerhead hatchlings,
Their noses below the sand,
Awaiting that moment when they breach their protection,
And dash over sand…

…And the MoonStar,
Calls them home.

"Winged Poet"

Low hanging cloud bank swallow shooting star,
In the thin inky line just over the horizon,
In a quiet August darkness,
Oil paint smoky rings of galaxies,
Spinning new colors, unknown to human eyes,
With your fingers,
Until the richness of the nebula comes through on the canvas,
And that smile,
That smile…

…It lines your beautiful face;

A netting of ethereal cloth,
We walk through the smoke that burns of emotional haze,
A precipitation that gurgles like fire set to sage,
May burn the eyes and affect the lungs,
Yet,
Onward the journey unfolds;

The diamas regns will come,
As sure as life exists,
But neither does the rain remain,
Where the love of God persists;

Fly, oh visionary,
Winged poet, breathe,
For Your light in which we are humbled,
It is for Your light…

…That we can see.

"She Moon"

Abloom, afire, a beacon, higher,
The Moon, aglow, agave, spire,
It lift, it pulls the tidal wire,
Striking with awe, and eyes inspired,
Flutter with the flaxen light,
Like a sea of liquid gold;

Behold,
These celestial mechanics,
The laws of the heavens,
Influence gravitationally,
Persuade the ocean, leaven,
To increase its rich...

...And gentle flow.

"Loggerheads"

It is still, yet not in this heart,
A bramble of wind toils in the gust,
Carry sea salt through the sea oat,
Carry dreams and forlorn whimsy,
Walking before dawn,
On a beach known at this hour,
Only by my adjusted, weary eyes,
And those of my Daughter,
Searching for signs,
Searching with my Daughter,
The cycle of eternity,
Of life,
In the buried nest on top of a vegetated dune,
Loggerheads...

...It is still here in the darkness,
Yet not in this heart.

"Prayer Stars"

The night as the moon wanes,
Dissolved in the west,
A blackness emerges,
As the satellite sets,
This blackness a fine cloth,
With sparkles on its vest,
Each star a prayerful memory,
For those for whom we've wept;

If the planets could reach their gaseous hands across,
And place their fingers on the Rosary,
They would hear the MoonStar in these beads,
Through their planetary hands,
Cradling handfuls of clemency seeds,
To spread in all corners of the universe,
Through a ministry of presence,
Of love,
And of light;

I myself have sown a million prayers,
Stars, each a grain of sand,
That pack together on this beach,
Under my feet.

"Shooting Stars"

Breathe the stars, their tails of liquid light,
When they streak across the field of night;

Breathe the glow that marks fire flight,
Prayers for the coin fountain,
My Love,
stay blinding bright,
For just a second,
For just one life…

…My Love,
And I in the limits of my temporary humanity,
And this temporary shell,
Ache with grave emotions,
As each breath is expelled,
Knowing that the faded trail in the sky,
Though seemingly empty,
Is a prayer,
Thrown into a wishing well.

"Mars Rising"

Long Jupiter and Saturn,
Have stirred their light into the sky,
While beyond the sea's horizon,
Another has yet to rise;

Patience and its virtue,
Are largely aligned,
With little to compete with,
She enters the stage on time;

Gold red, glisten planet, are you,
Immune to penetration of the naked eye,
Hiding your halo as you cross the stars,
Chasing your brothers across the sky.

"Dropped in the Wilderness and on Another Planet"

There is a way through the wilderness,
Though the debris remains irascible,
Though the debris makes this road impassable,
Though this road does not exist -

There is a method to maneuver through the madness,
To process each unbeatable sadness,
To own the mantle of courage on our frames -

There is a way with our axes and spades,
Like cutting a swath through the Everglades,
The fingers grow raw,
And bleed from contact with palmetto blades,
The lashes delivered from the underbrush,
Cause a flinch in the grace,
Though we travel on,
Though we travel forward,
Leaving our mark on an unkind landscape,
That otherwise considered us forlorn.

"The Dolphin"

A language, all their own, written in water books,
Water words on reeds of salt and air,
Water roads to lead their family,
Through a playful atmosphere.

"The Spirit From the Stardust Rise"

As with the galaxies within our eyes...

...We are brilliant fragments of light and sound,
Our cells encased in stardust found,
Like chandeliers of crystal and glass,
A million pieces through which the suns pass,
Radiating,
Illuminating,
Elevating...

...Every fleck of golden flesh,
The soul within the human mesh...

...Fulfills its holy vow.

"Human Sand"

A drop of sand on the beach of the Milky Way,
What galaxies are these,
Trapped in the spherical sheath of a tear,
Or wrapped into the capsule of another year,
How lovely do the shards of shells dance,
Chiseling against each other,
And ground down into human sand.

"Grief Harbor"

The toll it takes is deafening,
Blurring in its cruelty,
Speechless in the mentioning,
Paralyzing and taut,
No matter the movement,
No matter the momentum,
Always it, the Grief Harbor...

...Like a crying rock in the stomach,
Calls;

A ship well-built was meant to sail,
To leave the safety of its dockside nest,
A ship well intentioned and provisioned,
Was meant to face the ocean tempest,
No matter the current nor blistering tide,
Never caught without sails,
Nor with no place to hide,
Gripping the wheel, and sailing it blind,
He slams into explosive waves,
That erupt across his eyes,
Crossing the endless frontier,
Knowing no distance nor time,
Could ever shake the hold of Grief Harbor,
That sails along with him...

...In his heart,
In his skin,
Within his soul...

...Where his heartache resides.

"Only One Breath Brings Relief"

This, the furnishings of a prison cell,
Concrete bed and wishing well,
A life sentence in a brittle shell,
I grieve,
I grieve,
I grieve...

...For the lonely disposition and jagged array,
Of thousands of daily obstacles blocking our way,
It is a miracle,
That I can even breathe...

...But only one breath brings relief,
That final breath upon my death,
That I have yet to meet...

...For my lovely child, so young and wise,
Struck down and passing right through my eyes,
From the powerlessness of this world,
Is there no reprieve...

...No,
For this situation is not an event,
But a life sentence with no living end,
Until this life, well lived, through the grief,
Is relieved...

...But only one breath brings that relief,
That final breath upon my death,
That I cannot wait to meet.

"Every Second"

You slip into these moments,
Each and every moment,
In ways and mysteries that only you know,
In ways designed to touch my soul,
Even when unaware,
I find you standing here,
Here where I stand,
Every second of each day,
While the Pelican passes in the distance,
Am I unaware,
Of his purposeful, royal flight,
Causing the colors of the sky to re-arrange,
The sun to engage,
The angels to exchange…

…The grief rocks I gather,
For bricks of golden sunny rays;

Every second though I try,
Every second realized,
When I cannot feel you,
It is I who has gone awry,
It is I who has been distracted,
It is I who needs to be revised…

…Glancing back into this moment,
Where I find you waiting…

…Right by my side.

"The Weight (And The Intertwine)"

Trapped in a cave with no oxygen flowing,
Wrapped in enslavement,
The burden abounds,
Sapped of the will and with reflexes slowing,
Laugh and the pressure,
Exposed in waves of sorrow's sound,
Unfolds...

The weight, it was a grieving,
A grievance, it compound,
The weight, it was a thieving,
Of sacred, vibrant ground,
The weight, it come to swallow,
The weight is always found,
Rippling out from heartache,
Like no other heartache around...

...Daughter, through my confused apprehension,
and dazed in the trauma,
You offer intervention,
Crisscrossing the dimensions,
In this unfolding drama,
Lessening the tensions,
A resonance of sound,
A vibration of life,
Your life,
Your current life after your physical death,
Proves the miracle of Higher Light...

...But the weight...

...It may serve to break the bones of the spine,
It may press the human flesh through the gates of the divine,
It may fatigue, exhaust and scorch the heart and mind,
Or it may be fuel to reach across The Intertwine,
Where we live this day,
Any way that we can,
Holding hands,
In the collapse of space and time,
Where our laughter is our revenge,
And our revenge...

...Our shrine.

"Daily Reminder in the Storm Stream"

I have to remind myself each day that this is my life,
That this has happened,
That the nightmare of the ages has come true,
That it has come for me,
That I have been tortured,
In the worst possible way that a human can be subdued,
My child!
My child!
I scream into my darkness,
Where the emptiness forms a chair,
Where I sit for hours,
And empty handed, stare.....

It is not denial, but an overwhelming wave,
It strikes against good fortunes,
Each and every second of each and every day,
Where the dreams for my children,
Were eviscerated in a horrible accident,
When one of my children was physically killed,
And the other emotionally betrayed in casualty,
By a world that had given so much until then,
And then the nightmare happened,
And storms across my days,
This is not an event,
But a lifelong cage...

...I scream into my darkness,
Where the emptiness forms a chair,
Where I sit for hours,
And hours,
Stunned...

...Underneath the MoonStar...

...Skyward, I stare.....

"Stardust in My Eyes"

In those magical moments, when I can lift my head from the mire, from the rivers of grief that coarse through my veins; in those sacred moments when I have the courage and strength to reach into the mirage and apparent void that lay between us, and, for the record, those moments are every single moment that we have been seemingly parted; I yearn for you, lift for you, elevate in your name through my anguish and suffering, through the physical losses and towards the spiritual gains;

In those moments when I open my eyes to the glittering gold that stands just before me, at the end of my fingers, I stare straight into your eyes, catching the wondrous universe that exists between us, nose to nose, hands clasped in hands, parent to child, smile to smile, soul to soul; the swirling winds of love and light lift galaxies from your silhouette and from your blonde hair, and spins them around me in warmth and presence; in life;

I catch tiny soft crystals of stardust in my eyes where they gather in the corners; your stardust, melting into my vision and strengthening my resolve; for I am Father and I trudge forward; I will not be denied the standing I own beside my children; and my oldest child, now in your spiritual body, I am here; I wail for you; I scream out against this limited Earth for you; I embrace you in the peace I find in your arms, lifting all energy and reserve to stand in this moment with you...

...For you are alive.

"The Secrets of Our Lives"

I return to the walks of so many vacations,
To our beachfront where your childhood on display,
Emerges from the curtains of time and space…

…This time alone on the beach is ours,
Between the hours of sunset and sunrise,
Bands of spiraling arms of stars,
Range the darkness for you and I,
The rash of the Milky Way curves out over the sea,
And bleeds from the sky,
Merging into the blackness,
Where must there be a horizon line…

…And so sparks the music upon a sacred night,
With whispers rustling sea oat,
And shadows dance in moonlight,
We speak of turtle nests and Loggerheads in flight,
Of hundreds of evenings and hundreds of midnights,
Strolling in the darkness,
Laughter our golden bind,
And still, now…

…We sit here listening to the waves in the distance,
Water voices...

…And share the secrets of our lives.

"This Poison Light"

Burnt orange embers, umber,
A glowing parasite,
Dash and dart like bioluminescence,
Across the oceans of the Northern Lights,
It was infection,
It was poison, pox and paralyzing demise,
Wrapped up in a clever disguise,
In its complexity, it lay the universe low,
It, strip the mystery, rip and expose,
Every nerve ending of my spirit,
To the brightest rays of pain this world can provide,
With nowhere to go and nowhere to hide,
Not even can I shield the eyes,
For the light,
This poison light...

...It, emanate from inside.

"This Bridge"

Your feet, in this transition, across this bridge, they swept,
Stepping through your last moment in human flesh,
As you exhaled your last human breath,
Passing over this bridge,
Right through this bridge,
During that moment of your physical death...

...I felt your spirit,
Glowing,
As it flew through my ribs...

...Inhaling your first spiritual breath,
Stepping from that bridge and into,
Your higher life in The Continue,
With all that remains before you yet,
Seeing everything through crystal light,
And perfect heavenly sight,
Glancing gratefully to this bridge,
Embracing this sacred bridge,
Knowing, so well, this bridge,
Through which you passed...

...Is your Father.

"Of Our Lives"

With the strength of our hands clasped together,
Intertwined, engaged and tethered,
We are poised to punch a hole through the night,
Decorated with your Father's sea glass tears,
Star fields of remorse;

We, impassioned, and on the brink of brilliance,
A spear of coiled corded light,
Bladed with our thousands of years of journeying together,
The inherent strength we trust in the other's eyes,
That courage,
Unbreakable though currently weathered,
It will illuminate the pathway forward,
In the current statuses...

...Of our lives.

"Repairers of Creation"

Will you, reverently, improve upon this road,
Innately a good road, it is,
Yet open to ingenuity and creativity,
Failures and fumblings,
And opportunities and gifts,
To oneself, to another, to The Pelican circling above,
Though His path is no less a road,
Than it is the pathway of the soul,
To pound a greater gold from this gold,
The mission that peers into the gaps of growth,
Through love,
Love,
Love...

"Like Smoke Trapped in a Spider's Web"

Like smoke cells trapped in a spider's web,
Like tiny white dewdrops across the strategem spread,
These thoughts, like nails in a coffee can,
Rattle around my head,
Always searching for the sunlight,
Like darkness makes useless a precious gem,
I wake and, on these tiny threads, tread...

...Like smoke itself trapped in a spider's web.

"Cypressus"

Channeling cypress,
Branches for mourning,
Carving the trunk into walking stick,
Or used for river crossing mooring,
The rounded wooden cones have fallen,
Giving the grieving grounds a rugged flooring,
Lying underneath the quiet leaves,
Stubbornly exploring,
The every star in the swallowed ocean of this stranded sky,
And Heaven, all adoring,
Provides ointment for my eyes,
While cypress roots itself...

...Into my side.

"Wood Etchings With You"

We use words as dremels and chisels,
Phrases as wood burning whistles,
That scorch these etchings,
With contrasting sketchings,
Of dark and lighter lines;

We use poetry as a wood gouge,
Carving the stump like a field well plowed,
Surgical sculptures of metaphors,
Alliteration that paces accord,
Into etchings and clever designs;

We carve with an array of verbal knives,
And blend our love, and intertwined,
We create beauty from a talent divine,
And echo the love and the light that we find,
In each other,
Each time,
We invest in wood etchings of rhyme.

"Two Blooms as One"

We are together watering the garden,
Feeding the beauty,
Growing this beauty,
For both require investment,
Nurturing the beauty between us,
Cathartic action so little in effort,
Yet massive in its bridge building,
Feeding our channel,
Growing together,
Like two beautiful gladiolas,
That weave and bloom as one.

"Tomorrow's Memories"

With today's activities well in hand,
They, tomorrow's memories,
For now they are what will be,
Adding to each moment,
Each breath together,
A separate dream,
Though these are what we cherish,
When we look back at these scenes,
What is most important,
Are the current bonds together weaved,
For these are now the sacred truth,
Tomorrow's memories.

"One Sand Grain and Light"

I am a grain of sand of the beaches of a galaxy,
One piece of organic matter,
Blended with sparkling eternal soul,
Holding onto this human coil,
And wishing the fleeting winds of my spirit,
To take me home.

"Turquoise Light"

Is not, that within one's heart, fulfilled,
But a reflection of the Heaven, inside, built,
With dreams and hopes and loves and life,
And experiences that we each, to chest, hold tight,
It emanate from that beauty,
And fills the oceans,
With turquoise light;

She said, at youthful fifteen years old,
"The spirit of the sea speaks to the soul,"
And she praised the light within the water,
And she raised the light within the water,
This very special one,
My Daughter,
Brilliant, breathtaking, bright,
Who with her lovely hands,
And with encouragement from the MoonStar,
Fills the oceans...

...With turquoise light.

"Moon Star"

Powdered star dance, decorated with craters,
We see the fields of pocked laurels,
And shadowed canyons,
With the strain of naked eye,
Glow, yet glow in whose grand reflection,
The indirect light, yet brightest in the night sky, shines,
This Star of the Sea;

Mary holds within her hands,
The artworks spun into filigree,
Crowned with necklace of sea gems,
Gathered from the MoonStar,
Harvested from these sacred lands…

…Stella Maris
The Star of the Sea,

…Cradle me in your holy hands.

STORMING AMETHYST LIGHTNING

"The Sacred Hour"

From the sacred hour the heartache onward cascades,
And in each second in the aftermath,
The grief, it escalates,
Collecting daily on the footsteps of despair,
Building on a sorrowful atmosphere,
From which there is no escape...

...As I have been forsaken in the gallery of the dispossessed,
Where no oxygen dares venture,
Within the framework of my chest,
I, however, blossom,
A flower from a scalding fire,
For in that sacred hour there was also,
A miracle to take us higher...

...Into the realm of the infinite...

...Where the sacred hour blooms,
Where life thus continues,
Underneath the radiant blue moons...

...Of Exuma.

"In The Cauldron Of Emotion"

Coughing like a drowning rat,
Bobbing in toxic brewing sewage,
And gulping sulfuric ash,
Swirling in a liquid swill,
And water like lighter fluid,
That leaves acidic rash,
Upon the bridge of the mouth,
Each time you let the air out,
Each time you try to sneeze,
Each time you try to clear out,
Each time you try to breathe,
Each time you try to peer out,
From behind this web of grief,
Each time,
Every time...

...And what would this deceive...

...Should the rat learn how to swim.

"A Fissure's Mirage"

The first truth is living torture,
The second truth an enlightened fixture,
The third truth is salvation,
And the total truth is the full picture,
We are as one if we breathe the intent,
This family and its love and light mixture,
For we are eternally together,
In this mystical blend,
Regardless of our current situation,
And our apparent fissure.

"This Heartache"

I am walking in a tunnel of night,
Feeling like a ghost in my life,
Like a scabbard without a knife,
Like a candle lost of light,
Like wings absent of flight...

...And so with this heartache,
I go...

...And so it goes.

"This With No Name"

I slept in the bed of my life in comfort,
Though knowing the world unreliable,
Humble the effortless nature of pure happiness,
Then I woke in an instant to a place truly unrecognizable,
Destroyed suddenly,
A grief stricken strain,
Flooded the cells of the fabric that holds me,
Smearing my soul with the most authentic pain,
No worse can one go through,
Than this with no name...

...My child, my child,
To hold you for one second,
No price too high in the exchange,
Can relieve me,
Believe me,
I reach through the borders of my human cage,
Just to touch your light,
Just to touch your life...

...Engage,
Engage,
Engage.

"Yet Another Day"

The dream that the dream found within dreams,
Another fog bank in the smoky screen of steam,
Alight,
Burning off the morning shroud, the day,
It opens like a metal mouth to feed,
Staring at the window of my soul,
For any signs of escape that it impedes,
For all of my happiness has been eviscerated,
And my happy life, obliterated,
My God, what and how and why has this occurred,
As I dive into the abyss, grievously obscured...

...Another day,
Falling into another day...

...Yet another day,
Has called me to my knees.

"In the Palm of the Other's Hand"

I have been transitioned beyond recognition,
Struggling through grief's chest deep perdition,
It is the nature of this situation,
A lifelong sorrow,
That does not require spiritual sedition,
To burrow a void into the heart's hollow,
Though hallowed ground be this...

...We rise in each morning in the palm of the other's hand.

"The Wardrobe of the Sun"

The sun disrobed its solar gowns,
Flares of blinding beams arrayed,
And laid them in the liquid seas,
Where the waves absorb the fire cloth,
In a rapturous display,
Churning the ocean into gold,
With white caps and a silver froth,
That explode when the beach catches each wave...

...And then there are these moments with the sunrise aflame,
Carry on, carry on...

...Into the frenzy of today.

"10 Austin, Jekyll Island, GA"

This, just another day in the duality; where the sour and the sweet collide; where I suffer great torturous grief and sail above the heavens as the recipient of miraculous contact.

An excruciatingly brave moment, walking a mile down the beach to our old sacred beachfront home, a home sold after the accident, that has been altered inside and out. This is the only home in which you spent all 15 years of your physical life. I need to see it, and the dune side of our beach, as it was, and not as it is now. So we stayed on the other side of the rock seawall that protected our beachside from tidal erosion. I knew you would do something special and felt your laughter brewing.

Then I saw two pelicans cruising towards us above the retaining wall. Cruising in from the south end of the island, glancing in the sunbeams. Of course. Pelicans. This, as we are finishing our next lyrical book centered on pelicans! I knew it was your doing. Awesome work, Kayleigh!

As they passed over our old yard I realized that they were not pelicans at all, but two sacred osprey flying low over our old home and dunes where you spent your childhood, landing on the trees above our home. I've never seen two osprey flying in formation together, let alone over our property or landing on our property. I dropped by the old house, courageously, for ten minutes just to grieve, and to grow with you, and Kakes, you do this!

"I can come here, Daddy, whenever I want, but I can't come here with you if you don't come. Thanks for the walk on the beach. I love you, Daddy!"

To the doubting eye, you will never understand. For those who see, for those who are awake, rejoice!

"The Angels of the Ocean"

Angelic ocean sprites, their bodies gleefully alight,
Spiral in the silhouette of lunar flight,
Diving in the deep waves like pelicans,
That swim below the surface,
A veil, though blend, and one with life,
Emerging to the surface and bouncing on the waves,
Below as above alike,
Just before they take to the air,
And through the cloud banks strike,
The angels of the ocean spread prayer seeds,
As many prayers as grains of sand upon this beach…

…That glitter on the surface of the night.

"Diamonds to Exuma"

Path exists if renown the lens awakes,
Dusting off the limits that every human takes,
More than wishing stones and more than simply this,
There are diamond structures that melt away the fleshy mist,
Exposing channels, the spearhead of the soul,
Marvel through the tunnel, an astral road,
That widens one's vision at its mouth of flowers,
Opening into a panoramic view of the ocean's soul,
And waves of turquoise mesh,
Capped with glittering gold;

But only if intended,
And only if devotion yearns,
And only if extended,
Beyond all that you have learned,
And only if apprehended,
Of all that you have discerned,
Only then you shall know,
The flight of the spirit stirred;

Riding crystalline diamonds,
Through the refractions of precious stones,
Vibrational and faithful,
A doorway to a higher home,
They exist within the forehead,
Not born of blood nor bone,
Hailing in the majesty,
This eyepiece of the soul,
I am walking with you in Exuma,
With this eye open...

...And with my eyes closed.

"Breathe the Sky Within the Tide"

There will come a time...

...As the last breath escapes me,
No fool of prediction contain not respite,
For when and the where and the how,
It ignores me,
Until that moment I pass into light...

...And then that time will have come...

...When I dive into your waiting arms,
And fly through Heaven's color wheels,
The pulsing waves that build in the heart,
Release and expand into the reveal,
All of life's secrets lift, revelation,
Clarity comes to vanquish the surreal,
And here on the banks of Exuma Infinite,
Where space and time as one congeal,
With my Daughter by my side...

...The time will come,
When we wade out into turquoise waters,
And I, like you, breathe the sky within the tide.

"One Dimension As All"

Fluidly the dimensions, blend untethered,
Like melting vibrant oil paints radiate,
Mixing effortlessly together,
Earth, sun, moon and heavenly sky,
Light-years within us,
Echoes traverse like tsunamis,
Like ripples across space time,
That never reach the other side...

...Frontiers of endless promise,
I see this love within your eyes,
We gather suns and satellites,
And stars and cosmos and twilights,
Trails of wet stardust like summer sprinklers,
Chiming in the marching charge of dusk,
Dancing through the water rainbows,
With a delicate delight;

Enlightenment, a constant evolution of the soul,
Riches beyond measure are no riches at all,
For the richest of us is he and she who hears the call,
And in the selflessness feel themselves full,
Journey here, once lightened of your load,
And swim in these dimensions,
For they find themselves, inevitably...

...In each other's folds.

"I Give You, Daughter, Permission"

I give you permission to enter my hands,
To hold this sacred stone with me,
And humbled,
Your hands will be within my hands,
Just under my skin,
Your spirit stands,
Within this shell like air in wind,
Within my hands,
And blessed akin...

...To the Pelican Himself,
As I let His spirit in...

"Threading the Beach"

He came with treasure,
One that cannot be measured,
Nor melted into gold nor steal;

He wrapped it with psalms,
These sacred and indelible songs,
And placed it in the heart of the spirit wheel;

No secret to easy discovery,
No need for needless suffering,
Nor lengthy angsty appeals;

For the substance of this gift,
The feathers from His wings He gives,
To thread a soft blanket for one's soul...

...He, arch the breeze in a solemn ascent,
He, breach the fields where the clouds never end...

...Will my eyes turn inward,
Turn upward,
Turn as the Pelican shadow shuffles in the corner of my eye.

"Perched on the Sun"

And the reality strikes me strangely,
That sucked the air from my lungs,
Reiterating, that my child was physically killed,
So young, so young, so young;

It is not that I do not know this,
I stare down this path every day,
But there are disassociated moments,
As if the remembering, like loose clay,
Dissolves, devolves, decays...

...And then its reality slams back into me,
It sucks the air from my lungs,
My little girl was innocently, physically killed,
At fifteen ripe years young...

...And the heartache bites and lingers,
The grief, in raw color, it stings, it stuns,
While I turn upward for intervention...

...The Pelican,
He smiles,
Perched upon the branches of the sun.

"Awe Inspired"

Walking with an angel,
Stunned, an awe settles like mist on a flower,
A human mind trapped in its logical labyrinth,
Let go;

There is no cause to think,
Feel the great divinity beside you,
And bless the air that she occupies,
Walking with her Mother,
Holding her Mother,
And lighting up her Mother's left side…

…An angel, awe inspired.

"Kayleigh Lights A Candle"

Each day, though we do it differently after the accident, we are together. You show us many different channels; just extensions of how we used to communicate and love one another.

As I closed down the house last night, as I do every night, knowing that in the morning it would be Mommy's 50th birthday, and another hard day in the duality, I very clearly turned off every light, blew out your candle and stood in the darkness and kissed your urn holding your ashes. I meditated in the darkness for some time with you and asked you to try to do something really special for Mommy in the morning, no longer smelling a hint of the candle now cold at the wick.

You assured me, "Daddy, I've got this!"

This morning Jess woke up to her first day as a fifty year old, without her eighteen year old Daughter in her physical body; heartbroken daily as each day comes. She also woke knowing the second truth - that Kayleigh has transitioned, that in her higher body she is the same kid, just elevated from an amazing, vibrant young woman, to a super amazing, heavenly divine young woman as she continues to mature; that she is present, current, active; that she is alive.

With that hope Jess walked over to light Kayleigh's candle as she does upon waking each morning. She saw that it was already lit, a candle that only lasts a few hours. A candle that had been out for eight hours. She felt Kayleigh's unmistakable touch down her left side hugging her and wishing her a manageable and blessed birthday! Jess scrambled to me and led me over towards the living room table that held Kayleigh's candle. Awe struck, growing with Kayleigh every day, I silently cried and smiled, thanking my baby for this miracle specifically for Mommy.

Whomever you are, the unawake, no, I did not forget to blow out the candle at eleven o'clock the night before. Yes, Kayleigh lit a candle for her Mother this morning. Yes, Kayleigh is living on both sides of the veil, if there is a veil at all. I know some limit themselves out of fear or disbelief, but that is a choice. How little we know if we are not awake. The Mooney4 are definitely awake. We would have it no other way.

Thank you, sweet child. I love you so much and I am so proud of you; so proud of your current, maturing life.

"Enlightenment"

An era again begins,
An aura of kindled hope,
Moons of kindness delight,
In a sunrise that never fades,
The warmth, effervescent, it plays,
Like a gentle wind, its glittering breeze,
Glistens through the soul,
Settling into our joints,
And breathing through our skin.

"Loved Beyond Love"

The walls bare your paintings,
Your fingerprints, your portraits too,
The rooms fill with energies,
That shall never be subdued,
This house stands immortal,
With all that we pursue,
For this home is where the four of us...

...Continue...

...For now, grief is calling, and,
For now, its ponds are sprawling, and,
For now, the days are stalling, and,
The suffering, it goes on and on...

Hold me by the hand, Dear,
While I tremble and I shake,
Hold my frame together,
When the glue nears its break,
Hold us in the crucible,
Melting metals, grain by flake,
As we churn and mold this new day,
Into a lovely shape;

For always, light is shining on us, and,
For always this light is calling us, and,
For always I shall bring myself to us,
Please know, Sweet Child, that...

...You are loved beyond love...

"A Hummingbird, The Phoenix and The Pelican King"

(i) *Hummingbird*

Green breasted messenger, you dance amongst the flowers,
Radiating in your swift and gentle flight,
Imbued with heaven sent powers,
And dreams of magnificence,
Darting in and out of sight,
No cage of eye can capture you long,
Until you float upon the air,
In a frozen moment, like a long breath,
With a message, from wings you write...

(ii) *Phoenix*

For yes, she sent the Hummingbird,
This spiritual porter,
She is not what one may typically imagine a Phoenix would be,
She is, however, its strength, symbolically,
An angel of the Highest Order,
With missions and mighty responsibility,
She is tall and gorgeous, a woman of youth,
Who once emerged from the opportunity of challenge,
With passion and power and agility,
To a much higher truth,
Watching over her parents and brother,
In her angelic pursuits,
Always reverent to the Pelican King,
From whom she takes all cues;

(iii) *The Pelican King*

He sits upon the throne of men,
He the King of omnipotence,
The oceans under fingernails,
Galaxies know their significance,
But for his creative sway;

He, with perfect love and light,
The Ruler of divinity's hold,
He shall conquer the darkness of night,
And place within the human heart,
An endless fountain of liquid gold,
The Pelican King awaits your call,
If you shall find yourself desperate enough…

…Or simply find yourself longing to be bold;

(iv) *Spiritual Sensitivity*

I saw a Hummingbird,
Where before never this garden held,
It zipped in through the auroras,
And fluttered about the mouths of indigo bells,
Catching eyes with me,
As I sat upon the porch,
Crying for you…

The Hummingbird whispered,
A tiny messenger has come,
And from the furious flowing wings,
Rippled towards me a wind,
Filled with the essence of love;
And as this creature quickly darted away,

I was left feeling your hand in my hand,
Feeling your left shoulder against my right shoulder,
Feeling your left foot against my right foot,
Sitting with me,
Breathing with me,
Holding me tight enough,
So that I could momentarily breathe…

…Thank you, My Daughter,
For I have lifted myself into the realm where I perceive,
The greatest truth…

…Here, beside me always, you…

…And the doubters sit not in this garden,
Though they are welcome…

…But for us, and this communication, and these signs,
In the Pelican King's gifts, and intentions, and designs…

…I know the smell of my babies,
And I know the presence she divines,
For I know the scent of my Daughter's head,
And the light in which she shines,
And I know the fragrance of her soul,
It is overflowing,
Radiating…

        …With the Pelican's gold.

"Wet Sand"

Nose down on the earth,
Seeing the wet sand breathe,
The lungs expand and contract,
Through the organ of the beach,
And here I lay on my stomach,
To learn what it may teach,
Witness the orchestra dance about,
While watching the wet sand breathe.

"Our Immortal Cells"

Grief steeply seethes,
In its sting and deferential encasement,
Grief begets grief,
Fleeced by temporal disengagement,
While I find it hard to breathe,
Knowing this is not temporary enslavement,
I, at the surrealistic edge of forced belief,
Wonder at this life's cruel replacement,
What has come of me...

For it was effortless and a laughter's charm,
Swinging with my Daughter arm in arm,
For it was the precipice of a family in love,
At the edge of the cliff we were thrown off of,
Obliterating our lives in a sudden accident,
Is what it is now than what it was...

...I fear...

And The Pelican rise in the promise of the Higher Life,
He has elevated my Daughter into the circle of angelic flight,
As she sits beside me, though my eyes fail at sight,
She assures me in that same effortlessness,
That we are always together,
Swinging arm in arm,
That we are just in different body types now,
Though grief shouts with alarm,
She lowers into sunrise the blinding night,
Reminding me,
That our immortal cells...

...Are filled with Heaven and with light.

"Inches Implored At The Tip Of The Sword"

The sands of time dampened,
By the tears of a Father denied,
Robbed of all that he was becoming,
And all that she would have tried,
In the catacombs of endless sorrow,
He cries...

...Now shear vagrancies barter for his voice,
Accumulating weight on his back, brittle and brave,
He carves his way through a dimensional veil,
And sapped of human strength, he still prevails,
For she inculcates her Father,
With the truth of the Lord,
And hands him daily a basket of bandages,
And a holy weighted sword,
Forged for cutting his way through suffocating sadness,
Grief and its murk and its madness,
A fate fraught otherwise with fear,
Though he owns not the folly of the forlorn,
And, as a warrior would, here,
He matches calamity with a calmness and accord,
For faithfully he trusts his Daughter,
Who stands within the cradled light of our Lord...

...Teaching him each step forward...

...Just a few inches more.

"A Flock of Gold Finch"

Blooming morning light.

A yellow funnel of spiraling flight,
A dozen sunrises converge in the branches,
A sudden blur in the corner of my sagging eyes,
In the crux of spiritual circumstances,
Barreling in like a little biker gang of Easter peeps,
A flock of gold finch in the windows sing,
Psalms of levity, a reminder they bring,
To me...

...Breathe in the devotional intention,
For life, life is for the living,
And rejoice,
For she is alive, literally,
And lives in many ways,
Filling the air with a pack of gold finch,
As many as the leaves on this tree,
A cardinal sits atop the highest branch,
Just beyond my reach...

...Staring into my soul.

"Upon This Bridge"

Another board of grief to plank the abyss,
Building a bridge out of all that I miss,
Another board from thieves that stole your kiss,
I pound into place on this sturdy bridge;

Another board I breathe and churn from my fist,
And nail its intention with the hammer of my wrist,
Another board unsheathed from the wounded heart,
Arranged by convention so that I may live,
Walking towards you daily,
Across the breach...

...Upon this bridge.

"Ocean Eyes"

His regal nature evident,
His stature conveys reverence,
His eyes are worlds of eternity,
Through antiquity through modernity;

His glances always purposeful,
His teachings ever worshipful,
He walks us through these open doors,
Through lives to lives,
And shores to shores;

He paints the rise of morning light,
With His wings, the brush of life,
And loves his children unquestioning,
In ways too numerous for mentioning;

He never fails in human heart,
For this the core of who we are,
He perches in a sacred glow,
In the highest branches of the soul...

...And releases the wind in our eyes.

"Four Pelicans"

Three visible pelicans skirting the topography of the waves,
Choppy, gray waves,
Lazy waves,
Inconsistent and temped waves,
Fixing the adjustment of flight,
To the movement of the water,
Hugging the crests and dipping along the valleys,
Following the point…

…While the roar of the engine lingers on.

"Sea Angel"

Sea Angel, through the waves asunder, fly,
Flicker in the corners of our doubting eyes,
As ancient prophecies foretell,
You mark with lanterns the roadway in the sky,
Stars thrown into the mouth of a wishing well,
And arching away from this beach,
Across the wild ocean, rise,
Like a rainbow filled with bonfires,
Thins across the horizon's eve,
And,
Explodes into thunderstorms out to sea,
Lightning coughing in a cloud field canopy,
Reverberating flashes,
Hush,
A spectacular show of force,
In the dancing beams of fire strings,
While I brave with your encouragement,
These stepping stones to the eternity...

...Within me.

"Beautiful Day"

While on a Daddy-Daughter vacation, I was having trouble hearing you. We decided to go eat and we went to a few potential restaurants and, ironically, knew not to stop at each, hearing you laugh out to me as we entered each parking lot, shouting, "Daddy, no!"

I said to you, "do you want to go get pizza at our favorite pizza place?" I looked down at the clock in the car which registered as '5:55' – the numbers of your birthday, May 15th. I smiled, knowing that you were communicating down several channels simultaneously, and therefore, these signs were on purpose.

I went to this restaurant and asked for a table for two, as I always do, and explained that I was having dinner with my Daughter Kayleigh, who is now eighteen, and, in spirit. I told the waitress about you, your dynamic personality and the innocent car accident in which you were physically killed and transitioned into your higher life, as well as your constant presence and the miracle that we have never lost contact with each other.

We sat outside under a "WELCOME" sign, in the seats where we sat, the four of us, for dinner on our last trip right before your physical death. We have a picture of you and I under that sign. The waitress cried with me and felt you so strongly, telling me so; that she believed, and could almost see you.

As I finished dinner, I was choking on emotion, getting really weepy, looking out from that table, through the humidity, and remembering looking out from that exact table three years ago, remembering how everything was amazing in our lives; how strong and effortless our family was, and is.

All of a sudden, above me on the speakers, blared a U2 commercial, playing five second snips of "City of Blinding Light," then "One," and then "Beautiful Day," and then

"Vertigo." I smiled hugely since I heard in that quick commercial three of our songs, and in particular, "Beautiful Day," which you, significantly, removed from my phone a year and half ago. I explain this removal in our book, "Kayleigh's Voice." I have been compliant and have not heard it since that day, when you told me back then, "I don't want you to hear a 'Beautiful Day,' I want you to go make a 'Beautiful Day.'" So I have been waiting patiently for you to put it back on my phone or let me hear it somehow. I even once, a year ago, tried to listen to it on YouTube and told you, laughing with you, on the couch, "if you're not going to let me hear it, then I'm going to watch it!" And as I clicked the button and the video started, you promptly turned off the television! And now I hear just a few special seconds of this song in this commercial and it all welled up for me.

So, as the little commercial ended and I finished recounting all of this in a flash, then, all of a sudden..."Beautiful Day" played. The whole song. You finally let me hear it. I sobbed and smiled from ear to ear, holding your hand in your seat beside me. The waitress stood with me and I told her she had just witnessed a miracle and told her what Kakes had said a year and a half ago. She was in tears, and said gleefully, "well, Kevin, thank you! You have made a beautiful day by sharing your amazing Daughter with me!"

And that is that. Thank you, Kakes, My Love, My Daughter. You always know what I need, when I need it, and how I need the intervention.

And, I am still waiting for you to return "Beautiful Day" to my Phone. I know. In time...

"The Day's Last Fading Light"

Grains of sand glow like tiny diamond eyes,
Dust across the beachfront when the wind lifts from the tides,
Swirling sandstorms like faint and softened haze,
Add to the splendor of this wild and wondrous place,
As The Pelican, glide through humid, warm blue skies,
The ocean, bow in reverence,
The ocean...

...Lowers its face;

Dusk is steaming, meek and pastel shadows gleam,
Cast in the sunset like floral fabled dreams,
The spectral colors glancing westward in retreat,
Give way to the auburn blues and twilight wrapped in heat;

Night birds, cardinals, poppy red, they sing,
Fill the air with echoes, the gentle beauty rings,
Across the quiet beach fields and turtle cradle dunes,
While The Pelican swoops in, silhouetted by the Moon;

There is no reason to fret nor fear,
Caught lit only by the stars and the sacred sphere,
Stella Maris, She rises, She ignites,
Just after the day's last fading light,
While a figure cruises across the crests of waves,
Orchestrating guiding flight,
Though you may see him not...

...The Pelican...

...Is one with you in the night.

"The Light of the Ocean"

It lay silver and inviting,
Liquid laced with lightning,
A tidal zone igniting,
With the rumble of the waves,
Collapse and effaced,
Collected and erased,
Over and over again...

...It is glitter opal, whitening,
Across its angelic face,
Where her presence flows abloom,
Where I walk within the Second Truth,
Along this stretch of beach,
Where The Pelican speaks;

And turning towards the light of the ocean...

...I dove into its Moon.

"The Spirit is Jekyll Island"

And sacred Saturn burns the heels,
Of Jupiter who greased the wheels,
Of the lively heavens of the night;

Following the MoonStar shining,
Lighting up the beachfront lining,
The sea oat in the dunes have come to life;

Ship lights in the distance twinkle,
Though earth to sky conveys no wrinkle,
They are one blurred in the same in the night;

While you are both contemporaneous,
As well as sacredly simultaneous,
Illuminate two places with your light;

On the beach with Father, here you are,
Though also the sky bound MoonStar,
Love has no containment...

...We, we were right.

"Voices of Planets"

An eerie yet magical sound,
Waves that echo lightning,
Deep in the shallow of Jupiter,
In the auroras of Saturn's poles,
Where the planets breathe,
Exhaling storms that flash and glow,
Casting radio emissions,
To speak of all that they know...

...Like a thousand voices of angels,
Have come to call us home.

"Starlight"

Blinking, in the junkyards and the rustbelts of the universe,
Where the headlights of Jeep Wrangler burns aglow,
Catching shadows through the dune line,
And out into the darkness of an ocean's shore;

Illumination, across the fields of endless breath,
Elevation, expanding from the core,
Rising to the fleshy surface,
Harmonious accord;

And such radiance, it beam from every pore,
Starlight shine with purpose,
Out from where it is temporarily stored;

And I hold stars in the tears of my eyes,
These tears, galaxies where new suns are born,
From my arms you were cruelly torn,
In your physical norm;

Alas, though into starlight,
As you were transformed,
You stepped into your body of light…

…Renewed, alive…

…Reborn.

"Purple Tourmaline Moon"

Deep rash royal, flush with radiance,
Dancing brush, dash oil colors in vibrant gradients,
The contours of craters, fingerprints, finger paints,
A gathering of this family's sacred saints,
Harken glory in incorruptible grace,
And alters the momentum across the Moon's face,
So that it uniquely illuminates,
In a subtle green gleam of hope that breathes,
That emanates;

Blood orange fire gurgles in the mist,
Casting glowing steam,
In the mix,
That circumnavigates,
In spectral, aural shades,
And spreads, expanding its aura,
Across the moonscape,
In a heavenly sheen,
Purple tourmaline...

...Found only elsewhere,
Elsewhere in our dreams.

"Meditation"

Kayleigh, look skyward with me,
Here on Jekyll beach in the dark,
We stare in meditative contemplation,
As the canopy glistens with radiant stars;

"There are fields out there," you say,
"Full of everything that we are,
There are beachfronts and turquoise seas,
And universes within universes,
Within the Sacred Heart..."

The ocean tumbles in constant roar,
Here where we sit together,
On this hallowed Georgia shore,
Your golden hair flows southward in the breeze,
Your eyes convey a perfect peace,
Studying the path of my conveyance,
Knowing that with certain signs,
And certain patience,
Your Father will understand;

And so we sit together on this beach,
Deep in the darkness of the night,
I in my human flesh,
And you in your flesh of light,
Meditating together...

...And teaching me the meaning of life.

"The Vigilant Pelican"

The Pelican opens his wings and closes out the day,
He takes another stroke and the night is wiped away,
He banks across the Eastern sea and sunrise awakes,
He swoops Westward aloft and brings the dusk in his wake,
He moors the horizon in the crux of the midday,
And takes to the sky with vigilance while the sleepers lay,
Minutes to midnight where fear is testing faith,
Holding this beach under wing and in His claim,
For those of us,
Those of us...

...Who sing His praise.

THE FLIGHT OF THE ASTRA SPIRIT STIRRED

"We Are Walking in Exuma Tonight, Daddy!"

Calling me back toward meditation,
Knowing the distraction of strain has lowered the eyes,
From moment to minute,
Seconds long, or an hour or two to finish;

Marvel at the nebula we know exists,
Beyond the limits of our sight,
Yet trapped within these lenses,
I intend to feel my way to you,
As you are here,
Coming in and out of view;

I want to see you fully in your angelic state,
I don't care if it burns out my retina,
I don't care if it blinds my eyes,
To see your million points of light,
To see you dressed up in the divine,
Would be worth any outcome,
Any disablement of any kind;

"Daddy," you said,
"Look to the Moon if you are lost,
She holds all power;"

I sighed, hearing you,
And promising you this truth;

"Daddy," you continued,
We are walking in Exuma tonight,
While sitting on this familiar Georgia beach;"

And I smiled, seeing you,
And promised you this too…

"Purple Full Moon"

A royal glow dawned upon the Full Moon tide,
The celestial satellite dressed in violet light, rise,
Casting lavender radiance,
Down through the coiled blackness of night,
Glinting off of the constancy of fluctuating waves,
Like the heavens themselves orchestrated praise,
For the angel whose footprints grace these shores,
Having walked back and forth through revolving doors,
A guardian as constant as the waves and wind that glide,
Blessed by a purple Full Moon tide.

"Angel Aura Opalite Ocean"

The sea it sheen like angel aura opalite,
Purple silver, aqua blue and shiny sparkling white,
Dancing waves roll in the glitter and the gold,
Glancing in the moonlight deeply in the ocean's fold;

These the spinning rainbows swirling from her fingers,
As she dips her hands in the oil paintings of the soul,
No canvas without the artist shall this color know,
No canvas without the artist shall this color know;

She blazes sunbursts on this ocean canvas…

…While swimming in its glow.

"This Grand Spectacle"

Awash in the rivers of glitter and sunbursts,
Awake and alive, with no fears to unload,
I travel the breath of the universe streaming,
Expanding the limitless scenes of the soul...

...And aloft, my wings, bedded and soft,
Glide across horizons...

...In this grand spectacle.

"Before Day"

With the first signs of daylight color emerging,
I sit beside this stubborn nest,
Morning will soon squander the ripe darkness,
With its vibrant display of sunrise;

Golden reds and flashy orange dreams,
Blasting the lunar-like landscape here,
With a warm and bright solar light,
a new day,
Another day begins,
Without you in your physical presence,
Yet with you in your body of light,
In this perfect duality,
We sit,
Awaiting the new day in the darkness,
As the first signs of color gather in the distance.

"Electric Blue"

There is a sea that defies the eye,
Where crystal light parades the tides,
Like liquid lightning sparks a fire bloom,
With aqua rain...

...Electric blue.

"You Are The Miracle"

We are notes of music,
We are the purity of light,
We are ultraviolet in our reach,
Beyond the color wheels of flight,
We are the oceans,
And the stars burning bright,
We are together,
As sure as we are life.

"The Thesis of Man"

Though the beach sand looks like a field of white,
It is not,
Yet a kaleidoscope of colors grain by rain,
Storm by quiet by hurricane,
Sparking every color,
Every possible shade,
Though from a distance the long field is white sand,
It is anything but this,
As such is man...

...Like a complex set of individual pieces,
Cells, experience and thesis,
That frame this terrain.

"Pelicanus Nidus"

Along the calmness on the edges of Exuma Infinite,
He built a nest there,
Bedded with his feathers and His holy joyful tears,
With a vantage point high enough to view the children,
Wreathed and wrapped with silky strings of rainbows,
And clouds twisted into sacred twine,
He perched upon this thunderous horizon,
Where the sun perpetually shines;

She walked the beaches within the glory of the tapestry of souls,
She drew her Father across the dimensions,
And took him by the hand through these lovely folds,
For now is where the heart sings,
For now is where the heart grows,
They do not need to wait for his transition,
To be together in this home;

The wise and regal seabird with the ever watchful eye,
His heart is fullest when his children actualize,
When the children in the selfless moons of compassion,
Rise...

...And so along the breadth and span of Exuma Infinite,
Where she walks with her Father any way that she can,
The Pelican blesses this constant communion,
Between this angel Daughter and this Father man,
Whose love is a reflection of The Pelican Himself...

...Whose love is the brickwork foundation,
Upon which the kingdom stands.

"When One Is A Ghost Of Himself"

When one is a ghost of all that he was,
Exertion, inertia and emotional sludge,
It cakes the skin like glossy, haunting shell,
A personal, tidy, capsule of hell,
The kind that makes the spirit crawl,
Once that spirit fell...

...No, do not with your eyes upon me judge,
No, do not with your voice impel,
No, unless you have toiled in this trudge,
Not unless you too have been compelled,
To live the nightmare of all that was,
And all that is daily lost,
In the afterglow of a child's physical death,
In the status of posthumous,
A man, this man, a ghost, so it seems,
Until, into Heaven,
Into Exuma Infinite he too will cross.

"Rainbows Torches"

We are the words that open light,
We are the breath, the breath of life,
Illuminating compacted cloud banks,
Like electric fire that sweeps the peaks,
And explodes upon the darkness of the night;

We are the messengers conveying light,
Conductors, conduits, couriers of life,
We breathe and the stars pulse in envy,
We breathe and the stars awaken,
And in the inky sea of blackness...

...Burn like rainbow torches...

...Brilliant and bright.

"The Stand"

I am currently an embodiment of cells of flesh,
While you are an embodiment of cells of light,
And just as my soul resides within this shell,
So does your soul within your body of light dwell,
For we are present and eternal,
A hand in the other's hand,
Changing body to body,
From spirit to girl to spirit,
And me from spirit to man,
Until I too return to my full body of light...

...And in the same body type then again,
As we do now,
Together we shall stand.

"A Lyric With No Ending..."

Producing a hurricane wind in his mouth,
In the shattering vocals of a grief fueled shout,
A man screams and wails and delivers his grievance,
Sealed with his soul and the sadness that feeds this...

...Powerlessness...

He is dauntless and faithful and damaged and pained,
Deep in each day devoted and drained,
Yet he would have it no other way,
Than contact with his Daughter,
Any way that he can,
And he communes with his Daughter,
In whose hands he lays;

The mind is a blizzard of shards of glass,
The tongue the tempest in the typhoon,
As the ocean collapsed,
He pounds at the skin that fleshed in the sky,
Punching and prodding and clawing to find...

...A way out,
Yet there is no way out,
Yes, there is no way out...

...No way out.

"Words That Should Never Have Been Forced From My Mouth"

Reeling, the courtship came upon a caustic road,
Where life's fragility has been mercilessly exposed,
A man, is a dreamer, evoked by his delight,
Walking without effort through the gardens of his life,
Until that moment that he is wounded beyond repair,
In a sudden tragedy shelled by grief and despair,
He weeps, he cries, he seeps, he wails...

...And claws forward through the mire,
And the debris field of his life;

He is left pitting his mouth against his mind,
Uttering phrases that sound so strange every time,
A funeral? Your eulogy? Your physical death?
Words that should never have been forced to be said,
A child, his Daughter, the love of his life,
A brilliant young woman of which he is proud,
And now in the accident's aftermath,
He staggers...

...With words that should never have been forced from his mouth.

"Turquoise Air"

Turquoise the air that swims in the breeze,
The liquid sky shines like opal skinned seas,
That bed down the earth in glassy waves,
And blanket the shallows,
Its luminescent face,
And silky, indigo sheets,
With angel prints and prayers and deeds,
Swirling her fingers in the waters within me...

...To stir me, now...

Awake.

"Smoky Ocean Dreams"

Drowned in the webbed gloss flora of a smoky dream,
Where the figures dance through layers of shifting steam,
"Daddy, hold my hands as I stand on your feet,
And spin me to the music that erupts from the sea,
For I am here, Daddy,
Standing on your feet,
Hear me,
Hold me..."

The shimmer that coated the air with a million sparkling lights,
Was the corner of your eye that glistened silver and bright,
Shedding golden beams throughout the room,
Like the ocean holds the glowing beams from the fullest,
brightest ocean moon,
For us, my Love,
Soon,
Soon,
Soon...

"The Distant Shores of Sea Blue Moon"

Electric deep sea blue moon,
Its face of foliage fully abloom,
Radiates, a carnival necklace of lights,
Lightens up the darker corners of the night,
Blessed and blushing, behold enchanting breath,
She walks, arm cradled in her Father's elbow,
Though they are embodied in different flesh,
For his temporary residence, human cells and bone,
A minor aberration to the fullness of her soul,
For she knows the pathway, the road to be assumed,
And leads him to his next step...

...Upon the shores of sea blue moon,
Attained only down the diamond road,
Seeing the colors through the lens of the soul.

"Light"

You fill the world with light,
With kindling bundles of love,
Touched by the sun, ignites,
You glow bright in the evening,
And bleach out the darkest night;

For you fill the world with life,
Through your human experience,
And now in your spirit's flight,
You hold my hand as the evening,
Fades into blinding night;

...And all of the world, it gathers to see your beauty...

"Is Eternity"

Your light and your love,
You've collected in our beads,
So gentle the touch,
Your placement while I sleep,
And when morning comes,
I wear these like a wreath,
Deep into my skin,
Your light and your love seep,
While my light and love,
Leaches into these beads,
As I brave another day,
A gift of my life I bequeath,
At the end of the day,
When I lay down these beads,
You place them to your chest,
And the heavens glow and speak,
For light and love,
This light and love…

…We exchange within these purple beads…

…Is eternity.

"Emerge"

The pressure presses the galaxies out of my pores,
Like one million shooting stars that ooze from solar soars;

The pressure fleshes me with a thinning reserve,
Breaking down the cells and blinding the endings of nerves,
Until in a slavishly spatial silence,
I release...

...And emerge.

"The Higher Life"

Forced in the innocent moment,
Happy, living vibrantly,
And so, with no regrets,
in an instant she packed up her life,
Her love,
Her mind,
Her emotion,
All of her best,
Her sacred light,
Her last physical breath,
Expelled,
Her first spirit breath inhaled,
And she passed into the Higher Life…

…Lying in her Father's arms,
In through whom she had just traveled,
Now sitting to his right side;

She said, "Daddy, do you see it?
Do you see it?
Do you see it?"
As she passed right through my flesh,
She marveled at the spectacle,
And the glory unfolding just for her,
A million lights flashing,
Shooting out from her,
And down every street,
And through every front yard,
And every corner of the community,
In the cradle of God's omnipotence;

She tried to show me what she saw,
A carnival of angelic lights,
An open doorway to Heaven,
And the radiance of the Higher Life,
But what it was that I could see,
Was my beautiful Daughter,
Lying in my arms in the street...

...But I felt it...

...As you elevated, our relationship extended,
As we inverted our love ascended,
As you took your first spirit breath,
Through your Father's ribs and chest,
We, our light blended,
One in an earthly mesh,
And now one in an angel's flesh,
Ranging out and spreading her light,
Walking hand in hand with her family,
Leading them,
Leading them...

...To the Higher Life.

"God Is Our Binding Point"

Where distance and time align within flight,
And cross the paradigm within oceans of turquoise light,
The glue and its radiance adhere to this joint,
And solidify this binding point,
That coils together,
Two brilliant, blinding suns,
Two cords of life...

...Joined as one.

"Elongate the Spark"

Elongate the spark,
Take that electric light where the wires cross,
And secure it by the cords,
Stretching it, guiding it, working with it,
Taking a spark, a second,
And elongating it out over time,
In which we commune across the dimensions,
In our quiet time.

"The Intertwine"

Electric pink ropes of lightning wrap,
Tying a blue fire bow,
The crossing of love, it expands and enhances,
The immeasurable range of the soul,
Standing together with eyes ever widening,
Sacred compassion,
The core of The Intertwine, behold;

A crack of red thunder relays a vibration,
It cups along waters that crest into waves,
A tapestry, dreams and the sea and its gardens,
And echoes of courage from the vocals of faith,
Sing like a chorus across emerald skies,
Flanked by Archangels and thousands of Saints;

And she, now the spearhead, her Father she leads,
As he maneuvers the physical world and his grief,
Always she brings him back to the center,
Where each of their pink lightning cords meet,
And she with such patience picks up her dear Father,
Each time he collapses and loses his feet,
Aglow with intention, a blue fire bow,
And tethered together...

...They illuminate in a perfect peace...

...In each other's soul.

"We The Living Light"

We calmly unleash, beseech and release,
And fervently ask and repeat the entreat,
Dreamers are dreaming,
While dreams are deceiving,
If empty -

We may lionize the latest rage,
While tinkering idly in our little cage,
Believers are seeking,
And seekers are speaking,
For many -

For many, though wisdom remains failed breath,
They march like lemmings towards predictable deaths,
Leaving their spiritless souls awry,
To rampage into the unknown,
Confused and untied -

Yet, here we stand with fact and conviction,
Documenting true lives of non-fiction,
For all the world to view, and in spite,
Of the doubters,
We are the light,
We are the light,
We are the light…

…Of the world.

"Love"

Love, its safety, a sanctuary, home,
A great temple constructed stone by gentle stone,
Stardust mortar and mixed with sands of time,
The foundation rooted in a holy mangrove of the divine,
Pulsing mycelium through the veins bright and gold,
Connected in the ever advancement of our beautiful souls,
With growth exponential,
Bound in our mutual intention and devotion...

...Spinning in our own galaxy,
A celestial sky ocean,
Focused nose to nose,
Eyes to eyes like two sacred satellites...

...Stronger together, and with perpetual light...

...We grow...

"In The Mystic Veins of the Milky Way"

We, the angels, the keepers of The Light,
Speak to the night sky and lift its holy tides,
So its oceans may wash amongst the souls,
That seek sacred guidance,
Staring up from this earthly home;

In this mission, there are many roads,
Weave the wheels of the star fields,
All tied by spirit cords,
Leading from heart to heart,
From shore to shore to shore,
Setting flame to secret lanterns,
In each person moored...

...And if the world, it disgorge and releases pain,
We will use its fuel for our strength,
And channel together toward our birthright...

...The bond of our eternal home...

...A million blended sunrises,
A million blue corn moons,
A million sunburst and sun flares,
A million fold of love abloom,
Sunflowers as large as suns,
That through the webbing bay and swoon,
And there within the mighty sway,
The pulsing beat of life along,
In the mystic veins of the Milky Way,
In the lines within our palms.

"She King"

She the chieftain, the crown not made of swords,
She never sheaths compassion as she roams from ward to ward,
Sacrificing hours others can't afford,
For the dispossessed, opening new doors,
For ennobled, the service she provides,
Is larger than her gleaming smile,
And a thousand miles high...

...For...

...Never more can another fill the soul,
No other chieftain known,
Like She King...

...Who has gifted out the stores of her gold.

"Faith, A Sturdy Boat"

I close these limited eyes,
And open from the forehead,
Down diamond roads,
That lead to the water's edge,
And a tiny wooden skiff…

…And Amergin, an invocation calls into the crippling night,
The spirit of Ireland within this man,
Part this storm with the blade of this keel,
And bring this ship safely to her land…

…And as I trudge the tropical tundra,
The chop of unheralded waves,
Sweat stinging my eyes,
Covered in salt fragments,
Brave the ocean's dragon,
Colliding with the maelstrom,
Swallowing the swords of panic,
That eviscerate my throat,
Gasping for quality air,
In the smoldering fires emitting toxic smoke,
I arise and clasp the armor upon me,
Like a loose and cotton coat,
And strike out across the unknown,
These twenty four hours of water road,
With my eyes affixed upon you,
In Faith, my sturdy boat.

"The Miracle of the Sun"

In the purest eyes, an illumination,
For the masses call through them,
For the masses age with ruminations,
That block the spark from...

...The sacred gem;

All roads lead to the light,
All roads breathe eternal life,
Even the roads in which obstacles bait,
All roads seed the next test of faith,
Do you believe,
Do you believe...

...And we without sight,
We without sight;

...She with whisper the wind presumed,
A vision supreme of heavenly bloom,
The indirect light like that of the Moon,
Has walked among us,
Where peace and love ignite;

For whom shall witness in one's heart,
Or turn away, remain apart,
For shall we not when need has won,
Yet with desperate love,
Comes the sacred-most One,
To bring for those who need it most...

...This miracle,
Of the mighty sun.

"I Am (Sea Glass)"

When I first entered the ocean,
A shattered vessel my domain,
In shards and sharp the pieces,
A broken bottle I remain,
Yet how soft the edges of sea glass,
Once the ocean has its way;

As I toiled in this ocean,
Dragged over rock and sand and shell,
Through the nights of oyster beds,
And the pains of living hell,
And the grief it daily slays me,
And resurfaces my shape,
How soft the edges of sea glass,
Once the ocean has its way;

No matter the softening currents,
No matter the friction of sea grain,
I am always this broken bottle,
A shattered vessel I remain,
Though the soft gems of sea glass emerge...

...Once the ocean has its way.

"Immortally Wide"

She is the ocean,
A blissful summer sea,
She touches the dry dimension,
As the waves merge with the beach;

She hugs the horizon,
With long, skinny teenage arms,
With an ethereal sky beckoning,
And sparkling in the hold of her charms,
She is breathtaking sunrise,
That blinds the delicate eye,
She is the glitter,
The diamond opal tide,
She is the ocean,
Endlessly deep...

...Immortally wide.

"Eternal Dream"

The proof of life beyond the flesh,
Where light once resonated within the human mesh,
Now flows unhindered with no shell nor seam,
She grows and glows...

...Awash in an eternal dream.

"God and NGC 2775"

The Pelican, He circle His domain,
From Cassiopeia to Orion's Nebula Flame,
From the sea of stars beyond horizons,
A flight seemingly impossible to eyes untrained,
Though He flies and He flies....

...Through deep enlightened space,
Beyond the reach of diamond rains,
And perches on a galaxy,
Known more for its features than its innocuous name,
With flocculent spiral arms,
And feathery natural veins,
His newest project,
Tolls the quiet star nursery age,
With countless, sparkling blue stars,
In the pitch of their youthful gains,
On a beach beyond the wonders,
On a beach...

...Sixty seven light-years away.

"Human on a Human Plain"

We the vagrants that vandalize this world,
We stagger at the gatepost where flags remain unfurled,
Stain the earth with acres of disdain,
Reach across the mountains,
To scorch valleys and great plains,
All in honor, in glory of His word,
As we bastardize His name?

With permission emotion, it engage,
Permission to be human,
To weep and laugh and rage,
For the time here, an elemental stage,
Births our collisions and collapses,
And our joys that are assuaged;

This debris field is not given,
It is earned,
And can be avoided,
If the heart and mind are spurned,
There are many who walk within the light,
They have held true to their value,
And all that they have learned,
Being human and here on human plain,
They can touch the feathers of The Pelican,
And in turn,
Lift higher in vibration,
Like a sacred sea bird...

...Stirs.

"You and Me"

Where the dry sand meets water,
Land meets the sea,
We walk into the crest,
Of all that we believe,
We walk up to our chests,
In the brilliance of this beach,
As two worlds mix together,
My Darling, you and me.

"Sailing Into A Golden Bowl"

Many the moments in spite,
Of grueling air, wind shear, its blight,
Washes the wounds with jagged glass,
For if ever there is ointment,
Could it be as elusive as the past,
It pass,
And pass,
And pass...

Forward the eyes have buckled though,
With the weight that grief has offered,
But if only the hour could release,
And the tears one by one form a sea,
Would it be enough upon which to travel,
In a skiff carved from the wood of a broken heart,
And hardened by the trials,
And the storms,
As they amass...

Yet will I drown if sailor's skill,
Has retrained these hands,
To set the ropes and fix the mast,
Sailing into the unknown,
Into the deeper regions of this soul,
Where the big country opens into a golden bowl...

...That all along, Dear Daughter,
Were your outstretched palms.

"Resonance of Light"

Swirling wind chimes crackle with life,
Squeezing notes into air on a winter night,
She is standing beside me full moon bright,
Singing to her Father...

...Through the resonance of light.

"Purple Shooting Star (For Jonah, From Kayleigh)"

Shrouded in mystery, the human eye in failure,
Cannot see the color bands, and cannot see The Savior,
Though there amongst the shooting stars a violet eruption,
A tail streaks the darkly night, with emotional seduction;

It was one from this Angel and one for this man,
No need to explain for those who wouldn't understand,
For faith is no folly and folly owns no faith,
For love is the conqueror of time and of space;

We live enlightened by the MoonStar's embrace,
We hear her voice and we see her gentle face,
We mourn the losses caged in physical death,
Yet we receive the miracles of her continuous grace;

And so it came to be on a special northern night,
He listened to her calling and lifted his sight,
Catching the song she gave him,
Wrapped in purple flaming blaze,
"Jonah, my friend," she whispered,
"I am by your side...

...Always."

"A Tidal Wave of Sunrise"

As the nebula smeared, auroral its paint,
Spread through the Heavens like the gowns of the Saints,
As silky as breath and as deep as the reach is,
Beyond the Out Islands and their vibrant beaches,
Flooding the universe with penetrating light,
Like a tidal wave of sunrise wipes away night,
She is glowing in this brilliance...

...Rejoice, for this is just and right,
Rejoice for she is living...

...In the higher glory of life.

"The MoonStar"

This, the MoonStar, in her sacred grace,
Gave birth to The Pelican,
In whose light she shines,
In the glow of her face,
The eternal divinity,
Full and bright,
An immaculate embrace;

There are few, though they exist,
Who are like the MoonStar Mother,
They are reverent and humble,
And assume the nature of her heart,
They are angels of the Highest Order,
Where love has found its lark,
My precious Daughter, Kayleigh...

...This is who you are.

"Bathe Within My Sea"

An aqua aura quarts spreads out from this beach,
In salt scented liquid form,
Filling up the earth's oceans,
With its ethereal reach,
Above its waves the mighty Pelican,
With wings like starry blades,
Banks upon the highest winds,
And calls across the breeze…

"…Come, embrace my solace,
Bathe within my sea."

"Fatima"

And, an audience that gathered, quieted,
All eyes perched upon the brilliance of the sun,
For, to them had been foretold a miracle,
And for them, the fiery orb around itself...

...Spun;

Ushering in a higher proof to support the faithful,
And as, with this, a new day has begun...

...Momentarily...

          ...And the world with its worldly distractions,
          And with its pitiless eyes...

...The audience melted back into its ways,
And the field lay barren,
Where the MoonStar's song was sung;

For shame, oh, glory, Saint Bernard, through the ages,
If the earth can breathe your claim,

"...*If you are driven upon the rocks of tribulation*...

...*If you are tossed upon the waves*..."

(Daddy, as you look to me,
Your Daughter, who is 'star-like,'
But not The Mother Light,
Remember, also, to look through me,
Aligned with, a pupil of, the great beyond)...

          ...Look to The Star..."

"Adoro te Devote"

Oh, bird of water, water of light,
Ocean nester, bread of life,
Sacred plumage, brown and bold,
And penetrating eyes of gold;

Ranging from the tropics to the temperate zone,
In medieval Europe, The Pelican sat upon a throne,
A supplemental symbol,
To the Lamb who led us home;

Attentive to the young,
Wounding its own breast,
Offering its own body when food is scarce,
As the children breathe His breath,
The Passion of The Pelican,
That conquers physical death,
Rejoice! Sweet, MoonStar, rejoice!
For your soul is awash in this light,
For your soul is awash in this flood,
As Thomas Aquinas once humbly said:

"...Lord Jesus, Good Pelican, wash my filthiness...

...And clean me with Your Blood..."

www.ingramcontent.com/pod-product-compliance
Lightning Source LLC
Chambersburg PA
CBHW011140290426

44108CB00020B/2695